CHAMPION SPORT

BIOGRAPHIES

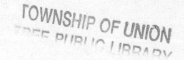

MIA HAMM

JOHN SHARKEY

W

Warwick Publishing Inc.
Toronto Chicago
www.warwickgp.com

Champion Sport Biographies: Mia Hamm

We acknowledge the financial support of the Government of Canada through the Book Publishing Industry Development Program for our publishing activities.

ISBN 1-894020-76-6

Published by Warwick Publishing Inc.
162 John Street
Toronto, Ontario M5V 2E5 Canada
www.warwickgp.com

Distributed in the United States by:
LPC Group
1436 West Randolph Street
Chicago, Illinois
60607

Distributed in Canada by:
General Distribution Services Ltd.
325 Humber College Blvd.
Toronto, ON
M9W 7C3

Design: Heidi Gemmill
Editor: Annis Karpenko
Series Editor: Joseph Romain

Cover and Interior Photos Courtesy of AP/Wide World Photos

Printed and bound in Canada

Table of Contents

Mia Hamm

Full Name: Mariel Margaret Hamm

Born: March 17, 1972, in Selma, Alabama

Height: 5' 5" (165 cm) Weight: 125 lbs (57 kg)

Education: University of North Carolina, Political Science, 1994

Married to Christian Corey, US Marine Corps Helicopter Pilot

Position: Forward

Career Highlights: (to Spring 2000)

- Two-time Missouri Athletic Club and Hermann Award winner, 1992–93
- Four NCAA championships with UNC Tar Heels (1989, '90, '92, '93)
- Three-time NCAA first team All American
- Three-time National Player of the Year
- Honda Broderick Cup for Most Outstanding Female Athlete in College Sports (1993–94)
- U.S Soccer Federation's Female Athlete of the Year for five consecutive years (1994–98)
- Gold medal, Atlanta Summer Olympics, 1996
- Gold medal, Goodwill Games, 1998
- Women's World Cup winner, 1999
- All-time leading scorer in NCAA women's soccer history with 103 goals, 72 assists, and 278 points over 91 games
- All-time leading goal scorer in the history of US soccer
- All-time leading goal scorer in international competition with 114 goals in 1999
- Awarded "The World's Best Women's Soccer Player of the Century" by the International Federation of Football History & Statistics (IFFHS) in 2000

Introduction

The young woman stands at center field silently acknowledging the thunderous applause of 90,000 fans. The roar makes the ground vibrate beneath her feet. She'd been here before, but never to such an enthusiastic welcome. With a modest wave to the crowd she speaks words of encouragement to her teammates and then turns and focuses on her opponents.

The young woman is Mia Hamm, the date is July 10, 1999, the event is the third Women's World Cup final, and the place is the Rose Bowl in Pasadena, California. Mia Hamm, America's most powerful soccer player, is about to lead her national team against the formidable Chinese team for the coveted prize of best women's soccer team in the world.

How did Mia get to be the best women's soccer player in the world? What were the circumstances and character traits that made it all possible? The following story will paint a picture of how a young, talented athlete arrived at this electrifying moment in her career.

Mia was born into an Air Force family that traveled to many different parts of the United States and the world. Her father was a fighter pilot and her mother an accomplished ballet dancer. Because the family moved a lot, Mia spent much of her time together with her six brothers and sisters. They loved to play all kinds of games, especially team sports. In order to thrive in her energetic family, Mia learned to stick up for herself at an early age.

When she was seven, Mia discovered soccer and she never looked back. Soccer became her absorbing passion. While still a 15-year-old high school student in Witchita Falls, Texas, she became the youngest player ever selected for the US national soccer team. At 19, she was the youngest player on the first 1991 Women's World Cup Team.

During her college years she took the North Carolina University Tar Heels to four National Collegiate Athletic Association championships. She scored more goals and is credited with more assists than any other college soccer player. For an extraordinary five years in a row, from 1994 to 1998, she was named US Soccer's Female Athlete of the Year. In 1999, she became the highest goal scorer in women's soccer history. Mia is at the top of her game and will undoubtedly go on to set further records in the future, many of which may never be broken.

For someone so talented and honored in her chosen

sport, Mia is surprisingly modest and self-effacing about her own accomplishments. Although she is a fiercely competitive player, she constantly acknowledges her lesser known, but indispensable and talented teammates.

Mia also recognizes that her success was shaped by important legislation that was passed in by the American federal government in 1972. Title IX required all federally funded schools to spend equal amounts of money on boys' and girls' sports programs. Up until then, sports funding went mostly to boys to develop their skills so they could play in competitive leagues and compete for valuable sports scholarships.

Since Title IX, the financial support for girls' sports has changed dramatically. Increasing numbers of girls are choosing team and individual sports to cultivate their skills and to realize their dreams. Although there is still room for improvement, women's sports teams are receiving more and more notice at the college level. At the Olympics, many women's events receive as much, if not more attention than men's events.

In the midst of her athletic success, Mia and her family experienced a tragic loss. Garrett, her elder brother, contracted a rare bone marrow disease called aplastic anemia when he was 16. By the mid 1990s he was very sick. He received a bone marrow transplant which seemed to help him fight the disease. But later he caught an infection and died shortly after. Devastated by this tragedy, Mia used her money and reputation to set up a foundation to search for a cure for this terrible disease.

As well as funding medical research, Mia's foundation also promotes and develops opportunities for young women athletes so that they can excel and be recognized in their chosen sports. She understands that much of her success is made possible by the support of others. This is Mia's way of encouraging and promoting the sport that has given her so much.

This combination of determination and generosity is what makes Mia Hamm such an inspiring and gifted athlete and role model.

Chapter One

In the Beginning

Today many people believe Mia Hamm is the best women's soccer player in the world. She has scored more goals in international competition than any other player — ever. She has won practically every soccer award imaginable, some of them many times in a row.

Mia has accomplished for soccer what Michael Jordan has done for basketball or what Wayne Gretzky has done for hockey. Many millions of children and adults in America and around the world have been attracted to soccer because of the talent, grace, and sportsmanship that Mia has displayed throughout her career.

Mia has come a long way from her early days in Selma, Alabama. When Mia was born in 1972 she was diagnosed as having partially clubbed feet. This meant her feet turned inward more than usual, which would cause problems when she tried to walk on them. During her first year she had to wear special casts to straighten out her feet. "Instruments of torture," her mother Stephanie calls the casts when she remembers the ordeal the little girl had to go through. "She had to sleep with them."

As her feet grew the casts had to be changed, a painful process that only stopped when the Hamms had to leave the country. Mia's father Bill was a fighter pilot with the US Air Force. He was posted to many different parts of America as part of his duties. When Mia was just over one year old, he was sent to the ancient city of Florence in northern Italy. Her parents, Bill and Stephanie, packed up Mia and her three older sisters, Caroline, Lovdy, and Tiffany, and headed off to Europe.

Italy was quite different from anything they had experienced in the United States. Not only was there a new language and culture to learn, there were no sports the family were familiar with. After flying, Bill Hamm's favorite passion is following sports. In the United States he followed the fortunes of his favorite teams and players in baseball, basketball, and other major league sports. In Italy there were no such games.

There was really only one game anyone paid any attention to in Italy, and that was soccer. The Italians loved soccer. It dominated newspaper sports sections, sports casts on TV, and casual conversations between neighbors. There were pickup games going on in the streets and organized leagues on the community playing fields. National and international games had millions of Italians glued to their radios and televisions holding their breath at every move of their favorite team.

As it was the only game in town — literally — Bill was soon drawn into the game too. At first he did not know what was going on, but soccer is not a difficult game to understand. The more he watched the greater appreciation he developed for the game. Soon he was taking the whole family to the local soccer matches on the weekends.

As the family sat on the sidelines watching the game, Mia's face would light up with excitement as she watched the players chase the ball across the field. Whenever the ball headed in her direction she toddled towards it as fast as she could in the special high-top shoes she wore to straighten her feet.

Back in the large apartment where they lived, her mother recalls, Mia would "just run up and down and up and down and up and down like she was practicing to get her feet right."

But just as the family was settling in and beginning to feel comfortable in their new country, Bill was posted back to the United States. After a short stay in Virginia and then California, the family moved to Witchita Falls, Texas.

Witchita Falls was a thriving community with all sorts of opportunities for family activities. It wasn't long before the older Hamm children were involved in various league sports, especially soccer. To further develop his newfound passion, Bill set out to learn all he could about the game so that his children would learn how to play properly. He started coaching and teaching soccer and read all the books on the game he could find.

Following the tradition they had begun in Italy, the family spent many a weekend at local sports facilities watching the older girls and their friends play sports. Mia was still too young to play organized games, so she had to watch from the sidelines with her parents for now. But she was developing a strong interest in athletics.

Because she was a small and rather shy girl, her mother thought Mia would enjoy dancing. Stephanie had been an accomplished ballet dancer before she married Bill. She had even nicknamed Mia after one of her favorite dance teachers. She wanted at least one of her daughters to experience the pleasure and satisfaction she had gained from ballet.

It didn't work out that way. Although Mia liked the idea of following in her mother's footsteps, she was miserable in ballet class. She found the "stop and go" teaching methods frustrating and she didn't like the dance outfit she had to wear. She left her second class in tears and never went back.

Mia wanted to play the kinds of games her older

siblings were playing. Stephanie accepted the inevitable and enrolled her in the local Little League baseball team for her age group.

At about this time, Bill and Stephanie Hamm made an important decision that was to have a deep effect on the family, Mia in particular. They adopted two Thai American boys. Martin was a few years younger than Mia and become the new baby in the family. Garrett was eight, three years older than Mia, and a natural athlete. Mia idolized Garrett and began following him everywhere.

"She stuck to him like glue," Stephanie said later. "She realized that it was OK to be competitive once Garrett come into our lives. I think Mia had this desire to bust a gusset and go for broke, and it wasn't until she got to play with Garrett and his friends that she realized it was OK to just throw yourself into that. He loved playing any kind of game, and she played any sport around."

At first Garrett didn't know how to handle this attention from his new younger sister. But that all changed once he found out what a good athlete she was herself.

Mia was so good that for a little while she was Garrett's "secret weapon." As she was small and shy, Mia wasn't the first kid to be selected for any pick game. But Garrett always chose her to be on his team. Then, at a critical point in the game Garret would signal Mia to go for a long pass or be in position to make a crucial catch. Mia, using her great speed, would be there to make the big play. This trick didn't last long, however. The other neighborhood kids soon caught on. From then on Mia was always included in the local games.

Mia loved to play and she loved to win. Her desire to win got so intense she would refuse to play if her side began to lose. She'd just walk off the field and go home. Her brothers, sisters, and local kids didn't put up with that for very long. They refused to play with her at all unless she promised to stay for the whole game. Mia soon stopped walking out of games. She learned a valuable lesson in team participation and she also realized that however much she wanted to win, she wanted to play even more.

Playing with Garrett's friends also meant she got to play with players who were older than her. It made her try harder, and contributed to her being even better athletically.

At one point Mia tried out for the football team at her school. Many of her friends were trying out, so she wanted to as well. She knew she was as good as, if not better than most of her friends. When she showed up for the first practice she realized she was the only girl trying out for the team. Mia just wanted to play. She didn't realize that football was considered a boy's game. The other kids knew her talents and wanted her to play too. She had no trouble qualifying for the team and even tried out for quarterback, although she ended up playing wide receiver most of the time.

As Mia got older she realized she was not going to be able to keep up with her male friends on the football team. The boys were getting bigger. She was still an excellent athlete and was always an asset to any team she played with. But with soccer she was a star, and that made all the difference.

Sports became a special tool for Mia. She was still very shy. Her family kept moving all over the United States due to her father's job. That can be very difficult for a shy kid, having to make new friends all the time. But Mia soon found that all she had to do to fit into a new school was to join a sports team.

"I'd join a team and make friends that way," Mia said. "Sports gave me confidence."

In the summer of 1982, men's World Cup soccer made a big impression on everyone in the Hamm family when it was played in Spain. The World Cup, the high point of international soccer competition, is played every four years in a different country. National teams from each soccer country (and that is practically every country in the world that can afford it) play against each other in regional competitions until there are only 32 teams left. These teams, plus the host country, play together in a final tournament. At the end of this tournament the best two teams compete with each other for the World Cup. Whoever wins has the right to call themselves the best soccer team in the world.

Soccer is the most popular sport in the world, with millions of players and many more millions of fans. Much to the amazement of soccer fans in other countries, sports such as baseball, football, and basketball have overshadowed any appreciation of soccer in America. Until recently, most Americans did not even know they had a national soccer team, let alone that it had not made it to a World Cup since the early 1950s. However, to the rest of the world, the World Cup is the equivalent of North American sports events like the World Series, the Super Bowl, and the Stanley Cup all rolled into one.

This lack of interest in soccer made it impossible to get any news or television coverage of the World Cup games in the United States in 1982. The situation was made worse by the fact that the games were being played in Spain. The difference in the time zone meant many of the games were played in the middle of the night, Texas time.

Fortunately for Mia and her family in Witchita Falls, they were not far from the Mexican border. Mexicans love soccer, so the Hamms were able to watch the games broadcast from Mexico City. The fact that they could not follow the Spanish commentary didn't matter. They all knew how the game was played and could appreciate and admire the plays and players.

After each daytime game, Mia and her siblings would all rush out to the nearest playing field to imitate their favorite players and the tactics they had watched on television.

By this time Mia had been playing for a number of organized soccer leagues, but the World Cup broadcasts gave her her first opportunity to see such world-class performances. It gave her much more confidence in her own game and motivated her to play as well as she could.

Mia's favorite position was right forward. It was the best position to score, and Mia loved scoring goals. Whenever she got the ball, her speed would quickly take her down the field towards the goal. She could either take the ball directly into the goal or could make perfect passes to teammates in better position.

It wasn't long before Mia was a force to be reckoned with in soccer games. While other players were still concentrating on dribbling and shooting straight, Mia could run down the field dribbling without looking at the ball. She seemed to know instinctively where other players were on the field. Mia had come to the point in her game where she didn't really care if she was the one scoring goals as long as it was her team who won.

Although she still loved most team sports, as Mia grew older she began to concentrate more and more on soccer. She played her way through the various levels of school leagues until she was declared a Texas All-State player. This meant she was considered one of the best players in Texas in her age group. Now she was entitled to play with other All-State players in various tournaments in her region.

One day, Mia's soccer skill was noticed by a man named John Cossaboon. He was the coach for the regional Olympic development team. At this point he wasn't really scouting for his own team, but instead was looking for potential players to recommend to college soccer programs. After developing in the college league, many players would be ready for his Olympic team. In 1984 soccer was not yet an Olympic sport, but the International Olympic Committee was expected to include the game in the near future. America wanted to be ready.

Coach Cossaboon was very impressed with Mia's talent. He watched her play in a game where she stood out among a group of talented players. He noticed her instinctive sense of the game and realized she was the best player on the field. She had speed and courage. She was not afraid to charge into a group of opposition players to gain possession of the ball or to shoot hard on net. Like all young players she was running on natural talent and still had much to learn, but Cossaboon knew Mia could be developed into a world-class player.

Cossaboon was so impressed with Mia that he

asked her to join the development team even though she was only 13 years old! He even told her parents that he was sure she would get a sports scholarship to the college of her choice, if she was interested.

Mia was amazed. She knew she was good but she never thought she was *that* good. She hadn't thought about playing soccer past high school. Now she was excited about the possibilities.

Chapter Two

The Game
and How It's Played

The possibilities that soccer presented for Mia and other players have grown tremendously since the game's humble beginnings.

Mia's favorite sport developed out of a popular rough and tumble game played in medieval England. Teams of men would try to get a ball to certain spots in a village or town. As there were no rules, many people got hurt, sometimes even killed, as they ran through the streets during these matches. Various attempts were made to outlaw the game because of the violence, but they never quite succeeded.

Later, during the 19th century, the British upper class began playing the game in a more controlled way in their all-male private schools. They saw the advantage of using the game to teach their children the values of co-operation, competition, and sportsmanship. Sportsmanship at that time was best summed up by the expression, "It doesn't matter

whether you win or lose, it's how you play the game."
It was during this period that the private colleges of
the wealthy laid down the "Laws of the Game," or the
soccer rules that are used today throughout the world.

For a period of time the game was called both "football" and "soccer," but "football" won out in Europe
and the rest of the world. "Soccer" became the name
of the game in Canada and the United States, distin-
guishing it from the more popular American football.

Soccer became so popular that by the end of the
1800s it was being played by all classes of people,
mainly men, around the world and had become
known as "the people's game."

Although there was a lot of prejudice against
women playing team sports in those days, there were
many popular women's club teams in Britain, Europe,
and America. The Fédération Internationale de
Football Association (FIFA), the international soccer
organization based in Switzerland, encouraged
women to participate in the game, but by the late
1920s women's interest dropped off. It didn't revive
again until the 1960s.

Soccer is still primarily a man's sport, but events
began to happen in the 1960s and 1970s to change this
situation. In the years following World War II in
Europe, everyone began to prosper and more women
had the time to take up soccer again.

The revival took a little longer to come to North

America, but during this period there was a growing concern that girls were not getting equal treatment in school and college sports programs. Most school sports funding went to expensive boys' programs like hockey and football. As a result, girls did not have much opportunity or support to take up sports, especially team sports.

This situation changed dramatically in 1972 when the American Congress passed a law on equal opportunity in education. Part of the new legislation, called Title IX, required schools and colleges to put equal resources into girls' and boys' sports programs. It took some time, but gradually the encouragement and acceptance of girls in sports began to take effect. By the time Mia was playing league sports, strong, well-developed programs for girls were emerging in major sports, including soccer, at the school and college levels.

One of the reasons soccer has become the most popular sport in the world is that it is very easy to learn and to play. Anyone can play, no matter how old or young, how big or how small. Also, unlike many other sports, there is no need for expensive equipment of any kind to play soccer. In fact many children around the world play the game in their bare feet.

The object of the game is to put a ball into the goal of the opposing team and to prevent the other team from putting the ball in your goal. Players can use any part of their body, except their arms and hands, to put the ball into the net. They can use their chests, heads and legs, but most goals are scored by kicking the ball with the feet. Putting the ball into the net is called a goal and the team with the most goals wins. It's as simple as that — almost!

Any number of people can play in a soccer game, but in official games there are two teams of eleven players each. Players usually begin the game lined up in three rows of three or more players. The players at the front are called "forwards" or "strikers." Their main job is to score goals. Mia usually plays forward.

Behind the forwards come the "midfielders" who are the first line of defence and who also feed the ball up to the forwards during play. The midfielders are often the most versatile players. They must be able to play both defensively and offensively at the same time. Often the captain of the team is a midfielder because a player in this position is in the best spot to see what is happening during a game.

The last line of players in front of the goal are called the "defenders." Their responsibility is to prevent opposing offensive players from scoring goals in their net. Sometimes a player, called a "sweeper," plays behind this line to act as an emergency defender in front of the goalkeeper. The goalkeeper plays mostly in the goal or penalty area and is the only player that can touch the ball with his or her hands.

All players can score goals, including the goalie, although a ball kicked by the goalie that results in a goal must first have touched a player of the opposite side before the goal counts.

The referee is the official who makes sure the rules of soccer are observed throughout a game. The referee stops the game by blowing a whistle when he or she sees that a rule has been broken.

The size of the field, called a "pitch" in England, is from 100 to 130 yards (91.5 m to 119 m) long and from 50 to 100 yards (46 m to 91.5 m) wide. The field is divided in half by a line running across the middle of the field. The sides of the field are called "touchlines" and the ends are called "base" or "goal" lines. In the middle of each goal line is the goal, which is 8 yards (7.3 m) wide and 8 feet (2.4 m) high. In official games, the goal frame has a net at the back of it to catch balls that go into the goal.

A regulation game is 90 minutes long broken into two 45-minute halves. There is usually a 10- to 15-minute intermission between halves. A game starts with a toss of a coin by the referee. The team captain who wins the toss decides which half of the field his or her team will start in, or whether they will start with possession of the ball.

Usually the first choice is what half of the field to start in. When a team is in their opponent's half of the field they are called the "attacking" or "offensive" team. The team whose goal they are attacking is called the "defending" team.

There are two important marked rectangles in front of the goal. The smaller rectangle is called the "goal area." This is where the goalie plays from without being interfered with by an attacking player.

The larger rectangular area around the goal area is called the "penalty area." If an offensive player is fouled in this area, he or she gets a direct kick, called a penalty kick, from the penalty spot 12 yards (11 m) out, directly in front of the goal. If an offensive player is fouled outside this area, the attacking team gets a kick on the goal, although defending players can try to interfere with the kick as long as they stand 10 yards (9 m) away from the ball when it is kicked.

Fouls are the most serious infraction of the rules in soccer. They are called by a referee, who determines how serious they are. Fouls can be minor, such as when a player touches the ball with his or her hand, or serious, if a player intentionally interferes with or harms another player. When a player hits a ball over the touchline, a player from the opposite side gets to throw in from the spot where the ball went out of bounds. If the ball is touched by a defensive player before a ball goes over the goal line, the attacking team gets a corner kick. This kick is taken from the corner of the field where the ball went out of bounds.

The most difficult and controversial regulation in

soccer is the offside rule. Basically, a player is offside when he or she receives the ball while there are less than two defensive (the goalie and another defender) players between him or her and the goal. It is often difficult for the referee to judge this rule, which can cause a lot of discussion with players and fans alike.

A more detailed description of terms and rules in soccer can be found at the back of this book in the glossary. Another excellent source of information on the rules of the game, as well as strategies, tactics, tips, and practice exercises is Mia's autobiography, *Mia Hamm: Go for the Goal.*

Chapter Three

Joining the Team

Mia was lucky to be growing up at a time when interest in and support for soccer, and women's sports in general, was growing. She would be given opportunities to play her sport that hadn't existed a generation before her.

Mia was thrilled to be chosen to play for the US Olympic soccer development team. Up until now she had played soccer for the love of the game; she now began to realize the importance the game could have in her life.

She had the chance to travel all over the country and to play with and against more experienced players than herself. She loved the stiffer competition. She began to learn more soccer skills than she would probably ever use.

In spite of her young age Mia was able to adapt to being away from home because of the many moves she had gone through with her family. Even though she was still shy and reserved, she knew that once she was on the team she would meet new friends and would feel more relaxed.

"Mia was quiet," said Coach Cossaboon. "She let her game do her talking, and she was always concerned with how the team did. She was ahead of the rest. We learned more from her than we actually gave to her, and it goes far beyond soccer."

It wasn't long before Cossaboon realized that if Mia was going to improve she would have to move on to an even more competitive environment. And he knew just the man to call: his old friend Anson Dorrance, at the University of North Carolina (UNC).

Anson Dorrance was already one of the best soccer coaches in America. With the help of talented players like Mia, over the next few years he would become a soccer legend. In college sports he was as well known as Dean Smith, the famous coach of the UNC basketball team, who had trained greats like Michael Jordan. Smith once commented, only half jokingly, that UNC was really a women's soccer college.

After attending and playing sports at UNC, Dorrance joined the coaching staff of the men's soccer team in 1976. When the university started a women's soccer team in 1979, he became the women's coach as well.

Dorrance learned a lot through his experience teaching the women's soccer team. He had a very masculine approach to coaching, which involved yelling and shouting at his players. He discovered that this style did not work with women players at all. Dorrance learned he had to let the women know he believed in them. He learned they needed to be encouraged, rather than screamed at, to do their very best.

He also learned that because they tended to relate better to each other than men, women developed a closer team spirit. As a result the women seemed to co-operate better on the field than men.

After Dorrance adapted his coaching skills, the UNC women's soccer team, the Tar Heels, started to win. Soon they were even more successful than the men's team. Dorrance found it so rewarding that he eventually left the men's coaching position to concentrate exclusively on the women's team.

The UNC women's soccer Tar Heels rarely lost. The team won their first National Collegiate Athletic Association (NCAA) championship in 1982 and won it four more times over the next five years. Due to his success with women's college soccer, Dorrance was made coach of the newly formed US women's national team in 1986.

Although soccer was becoming increasingly popular in the United States at the college level in the 1980s, in other parts of the world women's soccer was much more advanced. There were more developed senior women's soccer leagues in many European countries, and Japan even had a professional soccer league.

Dorrance knew that in order to compete successfully on the international scene, he was going to have to find the best players in the country for the US team.

The day came when Dorrance got a call from his friend John Cossaboon who persuaded him to attend a soccer tournament of under-19-year-olds in New Orleans, Louisiana. Cossaboon was so enthusiastic about Mia that Dorrance told him not to point her out to him during the game. If she was that good he would notice her right away.

Although his attention was fixed on a number of players, it wasn't long before Dorrance was only paying attention to Mia. What he saw impressed him beyond his expectations. Of that first exposure to Mia's soccer prowess, Dorrance said, "I'd never seen speed like that in a women's game. She had incredible potential and an uncanny ability to shred defenders and get to the goal."

Both coaches knew that Mia needed to improve her game considerably before she could compete internationally. They were equally confident that with the right training and challenges she was going to be a great soccer player. She had speed and natural ability. What she needed most now was to learn how to play against the best soccer players in the world. Dorrance wanted to see how Mia would perform against world-class players, so he invited her to a national team training camp in the early summer of 1987.

Mia was excited about the opportunity, but as usual, she was also apprehensive. How would she compare to the best players in America, some of them idols she had been following for years? How was she going to play with players like Michelle Akers, one of the best forwards in the world? Mia was still only 15. Many of the national team players had already graduated from college.

On the first day of the camp the entire team spent the first two hours lifting weights and doing other strengthening exercises. Mia had never worked so hard in her life. Then the team went out on the field to begin practicing! For the next five hours, with short breaks and time out for lunch, they practiced drills and played scrimmages. By the end of the day Mia was totally exhausted.

The next day Mia could barely move. Every muscle in her body ached so badly she wanted to go home. However, when she remembered what she had learned the previous day, she decided there was no way she was going to leave this team. She was awed by the calibre of play. She felt that she only knew the rules of the game. This was her chance to really grasp the tactics and strategy used at this level of play.

Mia was especially impressed by the intensity of the team. All the players were committed to doing their very best and expected everyone else to do the same. She was also in awe of the team's fierce desire to win.

This was the passionate intensity that Dorrance knew had to be present in order to develop a first-rate national team. Before, Mia had enjoyed playing and scoring goals because she was good at it. The national players made her realize that playing to win was the most important thing in her life, and she loved it.

The national training camp was a major turning point in Mia's young life. She was now fully committed to making soccer the central part of her life. When she returned home, her father remembers, she was focused on only two things: going to the University of North Carolina to play soccer for Anson Dorrance, and winning the women's soccer world championship.

Mia's dreams started to come true immediately. That summer, Coach Dorrance selected her for the national team. In August, she left for China to play two exhibition games against the world-class Chinese team. At 15, Mia was the youngest player ever chosen to play with the US national soccer team.

Although an experienced traveler, Mia was intimidated by her first experience overseas with the national team. She played her first international game in Tianjin, China, in front of an audience of thousands of cheering fans. Mia had never played in front of so many people before.

Introduced as a substitute at half time, Mia remembers the game only as a blur. She was not confident of her abilities in this international situation and was worried about making a mistake. In the end the US won a surprising 2-0 victory. Mia had avoided any serious errors. That in itself was an accomplishment for a 15-year-old playing at this level.

Coach Dorrance had put a lot of thought into recruiting young players like Mia. He believed a women's World Cup tournament would be announced in the near future and he wanted to be ready. He knew that by that time, many of his best players in the present lineup would have retired from the game and gone on to other careers. So, he was determined to recruit as many talented younger players as he could, to teach them his system. He wanted time to prepare the national team for the major opportunity he was certain lay just around the corner.

When Mia finished her first year of high school in Witchita Falls, her father announced that he was being transferred again. Bill Hamm was now a Air Force Colonel with increased responsibilities to take up in Braddock, Virginia.

It was a stressful time for the whole family. Moving was challenging enough, but the Hamms now had additional worries. A few years earlier, Mia's elder brother Garrett had been diagnosed with a serious condition called aplastic anemia which made it hard for his body to produce red blood cells. These are the cells that carry oxygen around our bodies. When we don't have enough of them, we get tired very easily.

Because of his illness, Garrett was forced to stop playing sports. Although he would continue to lead a normal life for now, his health had become a constant worry to Mia and her family.

Chapter Four

High School Soccer

When Mia and her family arrived at their new home of Burke, Virginia, they found a number of well-established women's soccer leagues. It wasn't long before Mia was playing on two teams. She joined the Braddock Road Shooting Stars, one of the best junior soccer clubs, in the fall of 1988. In early 1989 she joined her high school team, the Lake Braddock Bruins.

Motivated by her experience with the national team, Mia began to make serious decisions about her life. After talking it over with her parents and teachers, Mia decided to complete both her junior and senior high school courses in one year.

It was a big challenge and Mia was determined to do well in school. But she also knew she was going to have to commit more and more of her time to developing her soccer skills. What with training camps and away games, the demands of the national team were considerable. Mia was also determined to go to Chapel Hill and the University of North Carolina, where Coach Dorrance had already promised her a scholarship. Finishing high school early would allow her to move into the more competitive college soccer circuit sooner. There Mia would have more opportunity to hone her soccer skills.

That last year of high school was one of the most demanding in Mia's life and set the stage for many years to come. Between studying, practicing, and playing soccer games, there was no time left for socializing.

She was also anxious about joining the school team. She feared her teammates would resent her status as a national team member. But she needn't have worried. Her continual hard work and total lack of attitude won the respect of the other players, who also appreciated rather than resented her talents.

The Bruins were considered one of the best AAA teams in Virginia. In 1987 they had won the state championship, but then they lost it, by a tie-breaking penalty kick to their arch-rivals Woodbridge in 1988. In the 1989 season they tore through the schedule, winning game after game, until they hit an unexpected slump and lost two games in row.

The team recovered, however, and went on to win a spot in the finals, where they met up with Woodbridge again. It was a hard-fought contest. Mia was closely marked throughout, but the Bruins won the game by a score of 4-1. Mia had scored three of those goals, and the Bruins recovered the championship.

Mia did not have any time to celebrate or relax. She and other players for the Bruins immediately entered an international tournament along with the Braddock Shooting Stars, the second team she played for in 1989. They played against a Canadian team which they defeated 8-0. Denise Mishalow, the Shooting Stars' coach, commented after the game, "My job isn't too difficult. All I have to do is put them on the field and let them play."

After the successful tournament, Mia returned to Burke to finish her high school diploma. As planned, she completed her double year. Then she left immediately to play for the national team in Sardinia, Italy, where they held Poland to a 0-0 tie. Back home again, Mia spent the rest of the summer preparing to move to Chapel Hill and the University of North Carolina.

Chapter Five

College Champion

In the fall of 1989, Mia was facing a major change in her life once again. She was excited about attending the University of North Carolina in Chapel Hill, yet how was she going to handle this new challenge? University was much different from high school, and the Tar Heels were the most famous college soccer team in the United States.

To complicate matters further, Mia's father was being posted again, this time back to Italy. Mia would soon be farther away from her family than she had ever been before.

Fortunately, she was close to Coach Dorrance, and to Kristine Lilly, whom she had met when they both tried out for the national team in Louisiana. Although Mia was normally a shy woman, Dorrance and Lilly became like a second family to her, and helped make the transition from home to university a smooth one. While her parents were out of the country, Coach Dorrance became Mia's legal guardian and she spent many hours picking his brain about how to become a better player.

Academically, college was also much more challenging than high school. Mia had decided to major in political science, a demanding subject that required wide reading and numerous term papers.

In addition, like all college soccer players, Mia was expected to work out regularly, attend practices, and participate in all home and away games throughout the season. And to make her life a little more difficult, soccer was played in the fall at Chapel Hill, so she was immersed in the game and beginning her courses at the same time.

Mia was concerned about how she would fit in with the famous Tar Heels. Although she was an excellent player she lacked a certain confidence in her game. The Tar Heels had won three straight NCAA titles. The team was full of experienced, talented players, including Shannon Higgins, two-time winner of the NCAA Player of the Year award. Mia knew that everyone expected the team to repeat the championship again, so the pressure was on.

She needn't have worried. Coach Dorrance paired her with her good friend Kristine Lilly on the forward line and, with Shannon Higgins directing play from the midfield, the team blasted through the league games, defeating all opponents.

Although the 1989 Tar Heels were considered one of

the best teams UNC had ever fielded, Coach Dorrance knew they would have to work hard to win the championship. He still remembered the surprising defeat against the George Mason University Patriots in the 1985 NCAA championships. He was determined not to let that happen again.

The Tar Heels came up against their state rivals, the North Carolina State Wolfpack, in the Atlantic Coast Conference (ACC) finals. Although the Tar Heels had won the NCAA title the year before, the Wolfpack had beaten the Chapel Hill team in the ACC tournament. The heels had a score to settle.

The dramatic contest tested both teams' abilities to the maximum. The usually impenetrable Tar Heel defence allowed the Wolfpack to score three times. However, the forward line met the challenge. Mia and Lilly, the indomitable duo, scored two goals each and UNC took the game 5-3. In spite of being the youngest player on the team, Mia was named the Most Valuable Player (MVP) of the tournament.

The Tar Heels ran into the Wolfpack once again during the NCAA semi-finals. This time, they beat them 2-0, with Mia and Lilly each scoring goals. The team went on to play Colorado College in the final game of the tournament. For an amazing fourth time in a row, midfield star Shannon Higgins scored the winning goal in the final game, giving the University of North Carolina the NCAA title.

With a total of 21, Mia had scored the most goals of the season. Nevertheless, she still was determined to do even better. She knew she was considered an excellent forward, but she was less experienced defensively. Back with the national team during summer training, she drew on the experience of Dorrance and other coaching staff and concentrated on improving aspects of her game.

The increased effort paid off. Mia scored her first goal in international play against Norway in the first game of the season. That summer, the US national team went on to win all six of their international games. When the Fédération Internationale de Football Association (FIFA) announced that the first international women's soccer championship would take place the following year in China, the team felt they had been given a huge bonus.

Back at Chapel Hill in the fall of 1990, Mia found things had changed. A number of commentators were opined that the women's soccer team was past its prime. Some experienced players, including Shannon Higgins, had graduated and moved on.

The team started well but, towards the end of September, it received a rude awakening in the form of a 3-2 loss to the University of Connecticut. Mia had played very well and scored both Tar Heel goals. Several newer players panicked, however, and allowed some easy goals to get by. This setback ended an incredible 103-game winning streak for the team. It made the players realize there were no certainties in soccer.

Their next game was against the Patriots of George Mason University. The Patriots had been a formidable team in the past and had taken the championship away from the Tar Heels during the 1985 NCAA final tournament.

Recently, the team had not played as well, but still it was a threat. The Patriots played fiercely and held the Heels scoreless throughout the game. The Heels had botched a number of scoring opportunities and a powerful kick by Mia had gone wildly off the goal crossbar. It appeared the UNC soccer dynasty was coming to an end.

Then, with only 15 seconds to go in regular time, Mia intercepted a sloppy pass and streaked down the left side in a breakaway. In seconds, it was just Mia and the Patriot's goalkeeper, Hollis Kosko, who had played a tremendous game. Kosko came out of the goal in an attempt to cut down the angle. Anticipating this tactic, Mia slowed briefly, then faked. When Kosko moved in response to the fake, Mia quickly tapped the ball in the opposite direction. As she watched the ball roll into the back of the net, Mia knew she had won the game, 1-0.

The team mobbed Mia in appreciation. A new team leader had emerged and everyone knew it. Inspired by Mia's leadership, the team dominated the opposition for the rest of the season.

During the ACC final that year, the first-place Tar Heels were up against the third-place Virginia Cavaliers. Virginia played hard and controlled the play for most of the game. But the Heels stayed calm and, with Mia in the lead, kept relentlessly returning to the attack.

In the second half, Mia took a corner kick. She stepped back and gauged the players jostling for position in front of the net. With a decisive kick she spun the ball towards the goal. All the players jumped for it, but it streaked past the goalie's hands and curved into the top corner near the far post. UNC was ahead 1-0. Later in the half, Mia took another corner kick that was headed in by a teammate. The final score was 2-0. It was another ACC title for the Tar Heels.

For the second year in a row, the NCAA women's soccer final was played on Fetzer Field in Chapel Hill. The Heels played hard and easily beat their opponents. Everyone was pleased when they ended up facing the University of Connecticut Huskies once again for the final game. They now had the chance to even the score!

Mia was doubled-teamed throughout the final match. With Mia closely guarded on the left, Lilly scored twice on the right side to take the lead in the first half. The Heels scored four more goals in the second half to beat the Huskies 6-0, one of the most decisive victories in NCAA history.

Mia had dominated the game and, with 24 goals and 19 assists, had made the most points of the tournament — an impressive end to an impressive season.

After making such a significant contribution to the team, Mia was about to make another hard life decision. She gave it a lot of thought and discussed it with Dorrance and her family. In order to prepare properly for the upcoming world championship in 1991, she decided to leave school and put her studies on hold for a year.

Mia takes free kicks during a practice in June 1999, as Team USA got ready for a game against North Korea.

Mia dribbles past Germany's Sandra Minnert during a Women's World Cup quarterfinal match in Maryland in July 1999.

Mia holds the World Cup trophy during a TV interview in New York. Behind her is teammate Brandi Chastain, who gained instant fame for taking off her shirt in celebration of Team USA's win.

Mia tries to get the ball around Charmaine Hooper of Canada during an indoor exhibition game in Pittsburgh in October 1999. It was
the first game in a US "victory tour" series in which the World Cup
champs played a team made up of international players.

Chapter Six

The First Women's World Championship

Around the world, interest in women's soccer had been increasing steadily since the 1950s. Title IX had dramatically increased the number of women involved in the sport in the United States.

When FIFA decided to hold the first women's soccer world championship in China in November 1991, it wanted to take advantage of soccer's growing popularity and to increase its influence by encouraging more women's soccer teams. It also hoped to appeal to a potential billion Chinese fans. If the American team did well, it just might increase soccer's profile in the United States as well.

Although the American national team was elated about participating in the international tournament, it was not favored to win. Youth and college soccer in America had come a long way since the early 1970s, but it was still a minority sport with little presence in the media and not much of a national following. Other countries in Europe had older and better-developed club leagues and longer histories of support for national women's teams.

In addition, although the American team had done well in the recent round of six exhibition games, it had played against teams that were missing key players due to injuries. The national team had a lot of work ahead if it intended to reach the finals of the first women's world championship.

This wasn't the only disadvantage Team USA faced as it prepared for the World Cup in China. Many of the other national teams had large expense accounts; their players were on salaries that let them concentrate on the sport full-time. Team USA had little financial support from the American Soccer Federation. When the players traveled abroad, they often stayed in youth hostels or with members of the opposing team. This contrasted considerably with the US men's national team, whose members all drew excellent salaries and stayed at first-rate hotels when traveling.

In spite of these drawbacks, the US women's team was committed to their goal. The players put their lives on hold, postponed careers and families to follow their dreams. They were determined to play in the first women's world championship and perhaps bring the victory home to America. Realizing their dreams and representing their country to the best of their ability was more important than any financial reward.

The national team began its training with a series of intense, week-long training sessions in January, March, and April, followed by several exhibition games. This allowed the players to get to know each other better and to gel as a team. It also gave them a slight advantage, as most European players played in professional leagues and were not able to get together on their national teams until much closer to the tournament.

An added advantage was that many of the American players knew each other from Tar Heel days and were thoroughly grounded in Dorrance's coaching techniques and style.

In late April and May, the team traveled to Bulgaria and won six games against experienced European teams. Next they journeyed to Haiti, where the team won matches against other North American and Caribbean teams.

Then it was back to Europe and a series against England, France, Germany, the Netherlands, and Denmark. The fact that they only won three of their five games shocked the team. The confidence they had gained in the earlier tournaments quickly evaporated. They knew they were going to have to play much better if they expected to win in China.

During intensive training camps in June and July, the players concentrated on improving their performance. But when they went to China in August for three exhibition games, they lost two out of the three games. They did no better when they played against Norway and China in an exhibition series in the States, losing two games to the Norwegians and splitting wins with China for an overall 1-3 record.

By the time the team went back to China in early November for the world championship, nobody expected the Americans to do very well. Strangely enough, however, the team itself was more self-confident than it had ever been before.

Mia's decision to take a year off from her studies had been supported by her parents and Coach Dorrance. It was not an unusual practice among elite players who wished to concentrate on their games. Mia was gratified when her decision began to pay off. Coach Dorrance put her back at midfield, enabling her to improve her defensive skills. She soon learned how to disrupt an opponent's attack plans and use her great speed to go on the offensive. She developed a greater appreciation of the game and was better able to anticipate and set up plays that resulted in goals.

In spite of these gains, Mia was relieved when her good friend Kristine Lilly was invited to join the national team after another extraordinary season with the Tar Heels. Even with Mia away, under Lilly's leadership the team had won both the ACC and NCAA titles one more time.

On November 17, 1991, the Americans kicked off against a talented Swedish team in their first game of the world championship tournament. In a hard-fought contest, Team USA surprised everyone with a 3-2 win. Mia started in an outside midfield position, and made up for some early mistakes by scoring the winning goal.

The team went on to beat Brazil 5-0, Japan 3-0, and Taiwan 7-0 in a game in which Michelle Akers, the team's star player, scored an incredible five goals. By the time it reached the semi-finals against Germany, Team USA was on a roll and spirits were riding high. The Germans fought a tough battle, but the game ended up a 5-2 win for the Americans.

Mia and Lilly were tigers in all the games, scoring goals, challenging every ball, and wearing down the opposition at every opportunity.

While the Americans were battling their way to the finals, the Norwegians were doing the same, including an important win over the excellent Chinese team. It had come down to the final game between the two rivals — Norway and the United States.

Going into the championship game, the Americans were definitely the underdogs. After all, they had already suffered two consecutive losses to the Norwegians — and on American soil as well! With 65,000 cheering Chinese fans behind them in Guangzhou's Tianhe Stadium, the Americans attacked. The Norwegians returned the attack as soon as they gained possession of the ball.

The game seesawed back and forth. The Americans made the most of their few scoring opportunities. In a brilliant play in front of the Norwegian goal, Michelle Akers, surrounded by defenders, managed to head in the first goal of the game. The Norwegians pressed hard and a few minutes later evened the score. At half time the score was 1-1.

In the second half the Norwegians stayed on the offensive. The Americans did all they could to break through, but just couldn't do it. Mia did her best to set up plays, but they never materialized. As time began to run out, it became obvious the Americans were slowing down.

The Norwegians knew they were wearing the Americans down. They decided that if they failed to win in regular time they would take the game into overtime.

In trying to stall the game, however, the Norwegians made a serious mistake. With only five minutes to go in regulation time, a defensive player made a careless pass back to her own goalie. In a flash of speed, Michelle Akers crashed through the defence to pick up the pass then gently tap the ball into the Norwegian net.

Both sides were stunned as the fans rose to their feet in a thunderous cheer. Hardly believing their good fortune, the Americans rallied on defence and held off a frantic Norwegian effort to equalize the score. Then the whistle blew. It was all over. The Americans had won!

The crowd went wild. Meanwhile, Team USA reacted with a combination of disbelief and joy. The bench cleared as everyone congratulated everyone else. Shouts and tears were the order of the day.

As the defeated Norwegians left the field, a stand was brought onto the field to receive the first women's world championship team. Each player was presented with a gold medal. Coach Dorrance accepted a golden cup symbolizing the American victory.

They Americans had done it. They had realized their dream.

Chapter Seven

Back to College

When the national team returned to the US after their triumph in China, there were no welcoming bands or cheering fans. Few knew what the team had accomplished. Except for game scores, there had been no media coverage of the tournament whatsoever.

But the team themselves knew what they had done. They were the only American soccer team, male or female, that had ever won an international championship, and they were justifiably proud of their achievement. They had set out against considerable odds to achieve their dream of winning the women's soccer championship prize for themselves and for the United States, and they had done it. But no one at home seemed to care.

Back in the US, some team members retired from the team. They had reached an age where they needed to pick up lives that had been put on hold many years earlier. They wanted to start families and to develop other careers. For Mia, it meant returning to UNC to finish her degree.

With other members of the Tar Heels, she moved into rented accommodation in early 1992. She relaxed for a while and began to lead a normal social life.

When Mia returned to the Tar Heels in the fall of 1992, everyone noticed a difference. Not only was she older, she was a lot wiser. She was also stronger, faster and, through her experience in the midfield, played a much better, smarter game.

What transpired on the soccer field that year was one of the most amazing efforts ever, one that would go down in college sport history. Many observers called the 1992 Tar Heels the best soccer team in the history of women's collegiate sports.

During the regular season, the Chapel Hill team blazed through the league, racking up 22 wins and no losses. One outstanding feat of the season occurred during a four-day California road trip. Playing against first-rate teams, the Tar Heels beat Saint Mary's 6-0, Santa Barbara 5-1, Portland 6-1, and Stanford 5-0.

During the ACC tournament final game the Tar Heels were matched against the Blue Devils, a strong team from Duke University. Sixteen minutes into the first half Mia took the ball into the penalty area on the right side.

In previous years she might have tried to take the ball to the net herself. Now she drew on her national team experience. She slowed to distract the defenders and then sent a perfect 30-yard (27-m) pass across the field to Kristine Lilly, who was wide open on the left side. All Lilly had to do was blast it in and the Tar Heels went ahead 1-0.

In the early part of the second half Duke fought back valiantly to even the score 1-1. Then the newly confident Mia took control of the rest of the game. At the 30-minute mark, capturing a loose ball, she sent another perfect long pass to Lilly in the penalty area. Lilly relayed it to teammate Rita Tower, who blasted it into the back of the net to put UNC ahead 2-1.

Maintaining their aggressive style, Mia and the Tar Heels kept up the pressure. A few minutes later, Mia sent a well-placed 45-yard (40-m) pass to teammate Danielle Egan close to the goal. Egan headed the ball into the goal to up the score to 3-1, giving the Tar Heels their seventh straight conference title.

Although scoreless herself, Mia had three assists and had dominated the play throughout the game. Commenting on Mia's performance, Bill Hempen, coach of the defeated Duke team said, "She's probably the best women's soccer player in the world." He may have been one of the first knowledgeable people to make this remark, but he certainly wasn't going to be the last.

Shortly after, both the Tar Heels and the Blue Devils again fought their way to the final game of the NCAA soccer tournament. Duke was determined to even the score.

The game was played in heavy rain on a water-logged Fetzer Field, the Tar Heels' home turf. Duke quickly charged into the lead 1-0 with a header off a corner kick. This was only the second time all season that the Tar Heels had been behind in a game.

But no one panicked. The team went on the attack. Ten minutes later, Mia took over and played what some consider the best game of her entire career. First she drove a ball into the net from 12 yards (11 m) out. A few minutes later, while the defence was preoccupied with Mia, teammate Keri Sanchez scored from a corner kick. Seconds later, Mia captured a sloppy pass and scored again. The Tar Heels scored once more to close out the half with a 4-1 lead.

The second half started badly for the Blue Devils and got worse. To even the play, Coach Dorrance pulled Mia off the field, but it didn't make any difference. Soon the Tar Heels were ahead 7-1. With just over 15 minutes to go Mia persuaded Dorrance to let her back into the game. She was determined to play out the game with her close friend Kristine Lilly, who was playing the last college game of her career.

After the game Coach Dorrance said, "We don't enjoy embarrassing teams, but there's no way I would prevent Mia from playing with the person she admires most."

Mia went on to score her third and the final goal. It made her only the second player in a NCAA tournament to score three goals in a championship game. The Tar Heels ended the game with a score of 9-1.

In the process Mia had led the team to a perfect undefeated season and their seventh consecutive NCAA title. Mia went on to win an astonishing collection of awards for her efforts. She was the unanimous choice as the US Soccer National Player of the Year. She was nominated the ACC Player of the Year as well as the Most Valuable Player (MVP) of both the ACC and NCAA Tournaments. Along with teammates Kristine Lilly and Tisha Venturini, Mia was selected as first-team All-American. She also won the Hermann Award as the nation's top woman athlete.

Early in 1993, Mia was back with the national team training for a series of upcoming games and tournaments. As the world champions, Team USA were braced for stiff competition, and they got lots of it. It would be the high point of the season for any club that could beat them. In a three-game tour of Europe in the spring they lost 1-0 to both Norway and Germany. The American world championship victory in China had been a wake-up call to other top soccer nations, and they were determined to catch up.

The situation did not get any better during the World University Games later in the summer. The US national team was favored to win the tournament, and it reached the finals quite easily. But eventually they lost to China during the deciding game. The American players realized they were going to have to improve their game a lot if they were to stand a chance in the up-coming Women's World Cup.

Meanwhile, Mia returned to Chapel Hill and her final college season with the Tar Heels. With Kristine Lilly and a number of other veterans gone from the team, the 1993 season was not quite as exciting as the previous year.

In spite of the changes, Mia was determined to continue the Tar Heels' unblemished record. With Mia once again providing leadership, the team roared through the regular season without losing a single game. Although Mia was often double- and sometimes triple-guarded, she still managed to score 26 times in 22 games. And while the defence was concentrated on Mia, other Tar Heel rising stars like Tisha Venturini had greater opportunities to score.

Perhaps the most memorable moment of the season actually took place off the field. Mia and her housemates were at home one day watching a soccer game on television. When the phone rang one of the women went to answer it. She listened for a few minutes and then started screaming.

What they all found out at that moment was that soccer had finally been accepted as a full medal Olympic sport. Team USA would get the opportunity to play for the gold during the next 1996 Summer Olympics in Atlanta, Georgia.

Mia was overjoyed. Later she said, "Here I was, playing a sport and participating in an Olympic development program, and we weren't even an Olympic sport. For me, the Olympics was always the next step. What an incredible opportunity. You hear all the clichés, that it's a dream come true. Well, it is, for myself and for every young girl growing up who plays any sport."

In the meantime, there was the 1993 college soccer season to finish. Once again UNC faced their old rivals, a tough George Mason team, in the NCAA final game on Fetzer Field. A record number of fans for a college game, almost 6,000, arrived to watch the final contest. Most had come to see Mia play the last college soccer game of her career.

Although the Patriots played a hard game, they were no match for the Tar Heels. Mason did not even get any shots on goal at all during the first half, while UNC dominated the play and scored three times.

It was no better in the second half. Within minutes, Mia stole the ball from a defender, stutter-stepped past another, and broke towards the goal. There was nothing the goalkeeper could do. Mia blasted the ball into the net for the fourth goal of the game. Mia had also scored her last college goal.

With victory all but certain, Coach Dorrance took Mia out of the game. The game stopped while her teammates gathered around her in tears as the crowd went wild with support and appreciation. Although the Tar Heels won the game 6-0, as well as their eighth straight NCAA championship, people were only interested in talking about Mia.

Mia left Chapel Hill with an extraordinary college record of ninety-two wins, one tie, and two losses. She had garnered more goals (103), assists (72), and points (278) than any other player in the history of women's college soccer.

Mia was again the unanimous selection as the National Player of the Year as she led the country in scoring with 68 points on 26 goals and 16 assists. She also set NCAA Tournament scoring records for career and single-season points, and was named the recipient of the Mary Garber Award as the ACC's Top Female Athlete for the second consecutive year.

But true to form, Mia gave most of the credit for her success to her teammates. "The records are not important," she said after the game. "What it shows is the strength of the program and the traditions of the school. It's reflective of the people I'm surrounded with. They are an exciting and special group, and I'm glad I was a part of it.

"The goals and championships are nice, but the emotions, the tears, and the smiles on my teammates' faces are my championship."·

Always a true sportswoman, Mia is an example for athletes in America and beyond.

Chapter Eight

The First Official World Cup

Mia had had a tremendous college soccer career and had graduated with a degree in political science. Now she wanted to play soccer full time.

Even with all her athletic accomplishments Mia still had other goals in mind. The most immediate one was to rejoin the national team to further develop her soccer skills. The team began preparing for the 1995 Women's World Cup to be played in Sweden the following summer. After that, there were the 1996 Olympic Games to consider.

The women's national team finished the season with a highly successful 12-1 record. During the qualifying round in Montreal, the American team put on an extraordinary show by beating Mexico 9-0, Trinidad & Tobago 11-1, Jamaica 10-0, and Canada 6-0.

During the summer of 1994 the men's World Cup was held in the United States. It was the first time the championship was held on American soil. This brought more attention to soccer in America than ever before. Looking for stories about the game, the sports media finally discovered the women's national team as well.

When reporters also found out that the US women's team was the heavy favorite to win the Women's World Cup the following year, they began to pay serious attention. The team and individual members were profiled in newspapers, magazines, and sports programs. Suddenly, women's soccer was all over the sports news.

Because of her record and her natural good looks, the media was particularly interested in Mia Hamm. Although she recognized the value of the publicity, she was uncomfortable with the attention. She always emphasized that she was only a member of the team and not the best player by a long shot.

But the attention kept increasing, and it did do great things for women's soccer. Permanent training facilities were planned for the women's team in Florida. The US Soccer Association finally recognized the importance of the team and put all the players on a modest salary. This enabled them to concentrate all their energies on preparing for the approaching big games. Responding to the increased interest of the media and the American public, business corporations started sponsoring major soccer events and activities.

Mia accepted a lucrative endorsement contract with

Nike, the huge sports equipment company. Women's soccer and its players were finally getting the recognition they deserved.

The national team had a highly successful season in spite of some major changes. Anson Dorrance resigned as coach of the national team during the season. He was finding the responsibilities of coaching both the national team and the Tar Heels increasingly demanding. The many away tours were becoming stressful on his personal life. With the dramatic increase in attention paid to women's collegiate soccer, he decided to concentrate on his responsibilities in Chapel Hill.

The coaching reins were handed over to Tony DiCicco, another college soccer coach with considerable experience working with women's college teams. He quickly became familiar with the national team players he had been following for years. He already knew that the best way to coach women athletes was to stress positive encouragement, so he was able to continue Dorrance's coaching routine with ease.

Also, everyone was particularly concerned about Michelle Akers, their star forward, who was suffering from chronic fatigue syndrome. There was some question whether she could continue to play.

After the regular season was over, Mia made a major decision in her personal life. In December she married Christian Corey, an American Marine pilot she had dated for several years while at college. Following in her family tradition, Mia signed on for the life of a military wife.

In the months leading up to the 1995 Women's World Cup, the team played exceptionally well, losing only one game to Norway. Coach DiCicco placed Mia back on the front line where she bloomed as the team's best all-around player.

Later Mia said, "I worked really hard on my fitness, and I worked really hard on my defensive presence, and what I learned was that I was a lot more confident offensively because of that and I never was tired. A lot of my offensive confidence came from defensive success, winning a ball from a defender and then going forward."

Although Mia did extremely well and scored 19 goals and 18 assists in 21 games, the team still was not up to strength. A number of players, including Michelle Akers, were still sidelined as a result of injuries. In spite of the health problems, the team went into the World Cup tournament in Sweden confident they could retain their title.

They got a rude awakening in their first game. In a hard-fought contest against China, they battled to a disappointing 3-3 tie. The Americans were shocked. Their defence had not allowed so many goals in years.

In their next game against Denmark, they played well and were ahead 2-0. Close to the end, goalkeeper Biana Scurry was ejected from the game after a controversial hand ball infraction outside the goal area. As there were no more substitutes, Mia, as the third back-up goalie, had to go into net for the remaining time.

Sensing a final opportunity, the Danes pressed their attack and were awarded a free kick. With a wall of teammates in front of her, Mia nervously tried to find the right spot in goal. While she was preparing, the Danish kicker drove the ball directly towards the net. Fortunately, the ball went over the goal.

A few minutes later a Danish forward broke through the defence again and blasted a kick directly on goal. This time, Mia was in the right place. She made a great save and the Americans went on to win the game.

Mia admitted she had been scared to death. "The goal is much bigger when you're inside it than when you're shooting at it. I hope I never have to do that again!"

In the remaining qualifying games against Australia and Japan, Team USA played much better. Even though Mia was closely guarded, she was still able to make plays that gave Lilly and Tisha Venturini lots of scoring opportunities.

Finally, Team USA made it to the semi-finals to confront Norway. Of all the teams they had played since their 1991 championship, Norway had been their toughest opponent. In fact, they had won only one of their games against them during that entire time.

Right from the opening whistle the Norwegians went on the attack. They played a rough, aggressive game and 10 minutes in, scored the first goal. They continued to dominate the game, although the Americans were able to contain them.

In the second half the Americans began to play better. Michelle Akers was back in the game, but was playing injured and was not at her best. Team USA was not able to convert their few scoring opportunities into goals. Although they did their best they were held scoreless. The Norwegians took the game 1-0.

At the final whistle, the Norwegians went wild. After jumping and hugging each other ecstatically they wove around the field in a snake-like conga line shouting and screaming. The Americans stood despondently and watched. They had never experienced such a bitter defeat.

The Norwegians went on to beat an excellent German team in the final game to win the first official Women's World Cup. The American national team rallied to beat the Chinese team 2-0 and had to settle for third place.

Chapter Nine

Going for the Gold

The American National Women's Soccer Team were devastated by their loss to Norway in the World Cup.

They had trained so hard for so many years to retain their title as the best women's soccer team in the world that it was difficult to think of themselves as only third best. When the team gathered together a few weeks later in Florida for another training camp, they had some serious thinking to do.

It wasn't long before they had rekindled their spirits and their commitment to become the best in the world. It was time to move on to their next goal and leave defeat behind.

"We renewed our intensity," Mia recalls, "and geared it towards the 1996 Olympic Summer Games in Atlanta. Everyone committed themselves to being fitter, to being faster, to being stronger, and to bringing the team closer together both on and off the field."

From then on they were totally focused on winning the gold medal at the upcoming Summer Olympics.

The added resources given to the women's team by the US Soccer Association enabled them to spend all their time together. They lived, socialized, and trained together. The whole team would eat together and, whenever they could, they would go out on the town together to relax.

Team USA began their 1996 season playing a series of exhibition games in Brazil. Playing hard in exceptionally hot weather, they won three games and tied one.

When they returned to the United States, they headed into two games with their old nemesis, Norway. In the first game Mia scored the first goal and was the key playmaker in another. The national team won 3-2. In the following game, the two teams fought to a 1-1 tie until the final minutes of the game when Norway scored the winning goal.

Norway was still the main competition. Team USA was going to have to do better if they expected to realize their dreams in Atlanta.

Mia and the other players used their second loss to Norway to motivate them to play more aggressively. As the season progressed, they were winning all their games, until the team had a bad moment during a game with Germany in March. The US team was out in front 1-0. As Mia tried to outrun the defence to recoup a long pass, she collided with the German goalie. She was knocked out for a few minutes and had to be carried off the field on a stretcher. Even though the team went on to win the match 2-0, everyone was more concerned about Mia. During the collision she had sprained her knee and she would not be able to play for a while. Fortunately, the injury was not too serious.

The next game Mia played in was against France. That game turned out to be one of the most spectacular of her career. On another rain-drenched field in Indianapolis, Mia scored the first goal of the game and assisted on the second. Minutes later she drove in the third goal. Another teammate scored the fourth, then a few minutes later Mia scored the fifth goal. Shortly after that, Mia assisted Michelle Akers in scoring the sixth goal of the game for Team USA.

The Americans had held the French scoreless 6-0 at the end of the first half. In the second half the French team avoided complete embarrassment by scoring two goals, but Mia booted in another goal, and the U.S. won 8-2.

Mia had scored an incredible four goals and two assists against a top-ranked world team. It was one of her most remarkable feats and began to justify her growing reputation as the best player in the world.

By the time the team completed the regular season they had won 18 of their 19 games and the players were at the top of their form. And everyone was talking about Mia Hamm.

After two exceptional seasons with Team USA, the

news media lionized Mia as the best women's soccer player around. While she blended a remarkable balance of skill, speed, and power like no other player, she combined these talents with a sophisticated concept of team play. In spite of her success, Mia knew she would not be able to accomplish anything without her highly talented teammates. Although she stressed this in all the media interviews, no one was paying much attention.

The 1996 Summer Olympics were based in Atlanta, Georgia, with the soccer games placed in various cities around the country. This enabled a wider range of fans to attend Olympic events instead of only those who could afford to travel to Georgia.

The first game the Americans played was in Orlando, Florida, the city where the team had been training for several years. Twenty-five thousand fans, the largest number to witness a women's soccer match in US history, came out to watch Team USA play the first-rate Danish team. It was an exceptionally hot day with temperatures hovering around 100 degrees (38°C), but this did not slow the American team down.

Mia was in exceptional form and dominated play throughout the entire game. A few minutes after the US scored its first goal, Mia received a header from Michelle Akers in the penalty area and drove a powerful shot into the left corner of the net.

In the opening minutes of the second half, Mia collected the ball on the right side of the penalty area, stutter-stepped her way past two embarrassed defenders, and tapped a short pass to Tiffany Milbrett, who slammed the ball past the goalie. The Americans won 3-0.

The fans were ecstatic. Mia was the toast of the game and, along with her teammates, proved the Americans were true contenders for the gold medal.

"Every time she got the ball she was dangerous," Coach DiCicco said of Mia after the game. "She was the key player for us. Mia took the game over."

A few days later, the team was up against a well-prepared Swedish team. The Swedes had learned a few lessons from watching the Danes versus the Americans game, and Mia was doubled-teamed throughout the match

The downside of Mia's reputation was that now, more than ever, she was a target for rough treatment by her opponents. She was repeatedly pushed, tripped, and often knocked to the ground. Coach DiCicco complained repeatedly about it to the referee to no avail.

With seven minutes to go in the game, Mia ran into the Swedish goalkeeper. The clash left her with a badly sprained ankle. Play stopped as she was picked up and carried off the field by a teammate and a trainer. Although the United States won the game 2-1, their most valuable player had received a serious injury that could keep Mia out of the rest of the Olympic tournament.

With Mia on the sidelines, the team advanced to play the Chinese. Although the Americans dominated the play throughout the game, the Chinese played exceptionally well on defence and the final score was a 0-0 tie. Meanwhile the Norwegians, off to a slow start, had advanced to the semi-finals. The two old foes prepared to meet on the pitch once more.

After careful consideration, Coach DiCicco allowed Mia to start in this crucial contest. Mia's ankle was still giving her trouble, but she could play. Even playing at less than her best, she was still a threat, and the Norwegians would have to focus on her all the time. This might give other American players opportunities to score.

Following the example of the Swedes, Mia was heavily covered by the Norwegians and was subjected to repeated rough play throughout the game. She was knocked to the ground many times without the referee calling foul. With both teams playing as aggressively as they could, the Norwegians scored first 18 minutes into the game. Try as they might, the Americans couldn't sink the equalizer.

In the second half the struggle continued with the ball volleying back and forth across the field. With only 12 minutes left, Mia received a well-placed pass in the penalty area. As she charged towards the goal she was viciously tackled by two defenders and fell to the ground. Finally, the referee called a foul and the Americans were awarded a penalty kick.

Normally Mia would have taken the shot herself but, because of her injured ankle, Coach DiCicco sent in Akers to do the job. The fans sent up a roar of disapproval. They wanted Mia. Yet the coach knew Akers had one of the most powerful kicks of any player in international women's soccer.

The veteran player didn't disappoint her team or the fans. In spite of the Norwegian goalie's best effort, Akers drove the ball expertly into the back of the net. The game was tied. Both teams did their best to score in the final minutes of the game, but it ended 1-1.

As there could be no tie games at this stage of the tournament, the match went into overtime. It was now or never for Team USA. Judging that the team could use some fresh legs, Coach DiCicco started forward Shannon MacMillan in the overtime period. At the four-minute mark, MacMillan received a smooth pass from midfielder Julie Foudy and blasted in the winning goal. The final score was 2-1. The Americans were headed for the final crucial contest for the gold medal. In spite of her injury Mia had played every second of the game.

Four days later, on August 1, Mia and her teammates came up against the Chinese in Stanford Stadium. This was their final step in their quest to win the Olympic gold medal. As the Americans got closer to the final, the crowds had grown larger. But nobody was prepared for the 76,000 fans in the stands that day. The fans roared with appreciation the moment the team stepped onto the field. Banners, signs, and flags were everywhere. Every young face seemed to be painted red, white, and blue. There was a constant chant of "USA, USA, USA." The noise was almost deafening.

And then the game began. Coach DiCicco had warned the team to be careful.

"China is a very good team," he had told them earlier in the day. "In the group match, they played for tie. We can't expect that in the final."

Once the game was underway the team forgot about the past and the fans. They concentrated on the moment — and winning the gold. DiCicco was right. The Chinese came out aggressively. During the opening minutes, each side probed the other for weaknesses or momentary errors that would provide goal opportunities.

At the 20-minute mark, Kristine Lilly dribbled the ball down the left side of the field while Mia ran down the right, executing a pattern they had performed many times before. In mid-stride, Lilly sent a long pass across the penalty area in Mia's direction. Using her great speed, Mia dashed past defenders to meet the ball close to the goal area. Then she drove it towards the goal. The Chinese goalie made a brilliant finger-tip save and deflected the ball against the far goal post. Then it bounced back into play. While the crowd sent up a tremendous cheer, Shannon MacMillan appeared out of nowhere. She sent the ball under the goalkeeper's right arm and into the net. The US was ahead 1-0.

But the Chinese didn't let up for a second. They came back with a vengeance and took control of the game. Keeping the ball constantly in the American half of the field, they desperately strove to even the score.

Thirty minutes into the game, the brilliant Chinese forward broke through the defence towards the goal. Biana Scurry raced to meet her to cut down on the goal angle. In a play that marked her as a true Olympian, the Chinese player gently lobbed the ball over Scurry's head and into the net. Now the score was 1-1, where it stayed for the rest of the half.

During the break, Coach DiCicco drew the team together to offer advice and encouragement. Mia was still in considerable pain from her left ankle. She also was suffering from a strained muscle in her groin that was holding her back at high speed. Should she leave the game so as not to hold back the team? None of the other players thought so. She was too valuable even if she was injured. As Shannon MacMillian said, "Even if you're not hundred percent, the Chinese have to worry about you, which means someone else might get free."

From the start of the second half it was obvious MacMillian was right. Mia orchestrated the offence, setting up plays and encouraging her teammates. Then, 20 minutes into the half, Mia got possession of the ball. The Chinese defence came out to confront her. Seeing Joy Fawcett running past the defence towards the goal, Mia sent her a flawless pass that her team-mate picked up in stride. Rushing the goal, Fawcett slipped the ball past a frantic defender to a perfectly placed Tiffany Milbrett in front of the net. Milbrett drove the ball into the back of the net. Goal! Now Team USA was up 2-1.

For the members of Team USA, the remaining 25 minutes of the game seemed to last forever. But no matter how hard the Chinese played, they could not crack the American defence. With only a few minutes to go, Mia's ankle gave out again and she collapsed to her knees in pain. As the crowed roared its support, Mia was helped from the field.

Somehow Mia felt she had let the team down by her injury. But it soon became clear that what Mia had been saying all along was true. She was part of a tremendous team that could win without her if they had to. The team was also determined not to let Mia down and the players maintained their defence until the gun sounded to end the game. Team USA had won the Olympic gold medal!

The American players went wild with excitement.

So did the fans. While the rest of the team took a victory lap around the field draped in their national flag, Mia was helped onto the field by a trainer. She stood watching and waving at the crowd with tears in her eyes. In the stands were friends and family, including her brother Garrett, whose health was deteriorating. Mia thought about all the support she had received over the years, particularly from Garrett, who had helped so much to get her where she was at that moment.

After the award ceremony, the media clustered around Mia to get her reaction to the game. As always, Mia praised her teammates.

"This team is incredible," she said. "We all believed in each other and we believed in this day. From the beginning, this has been an entire team effort."

It was left to her teammates to give Mia the praise she deserved. Speaking for the team and for all her fans, Brandi Chastain said, "Mia impacts the game whether she scores or not. She tears defences apart. She is awesome!"

Chapter Ten

The Road to the 1999 Women's World Cup and Beyond

The success of the American national team in the 1996 Summer Olympics was a watershed for women's soccer in the United States. The publicity surrounding the Olympics and the explosion of interest in soccer created one of the sports events of the decade. The team was tremendously popular with the public and the media.

Mia Hamm became an overnight sensation. She was the darling of the media and she was bombarded with requests to do newspaper and magazine interviews, to appear on television, and to make public appearances.

Mia was not personally comfortable with all the attention. However, she knew that to increase soccer's profile, she and her teammates were expected to promote the sport by acting as teachers, role models, and ambassadors for soccer.

Wherever the team went, Mia was sure to be surrounded by awestruck youngsters wearing number 9 jerseys and begging for autographs. She gave as much of her time and encouragement as possible, knowing how important it was for children, particularly young girls, to have women role models to inspire them.

Meanwhile, Mia's brother Garrett's condition had steadily worsened. In an effort to help her brother, Mia began distributing information about aplastic anemia whenever she made public appearances. To find donors for a bone marrow transplant to help Garrett and people like him, she urged people to take a simple blood test. Usually a donor can be found within the immediate family, but because Garrett was adopted no one in the Hamm family had his blood type. Unless the right donor could be found, Garrett would not live much longer.

The family's hopes were raised when, after an intensive search, Garrett's birth father was located. He immediately agreed to be a donor. The resulting operation was a success. Garrett began to recover and gradually to feel more like his old self.

Miraculous as they are in saving deathly ill people, bone marrow and other types of transplants can also create problems with the immune system. Our immune system protects us when germs get into our bodies. When people get a transplant, there is the chance that their immune system will try to fight this new "foreign" material in the body. To try to avoid this, transplant patients take drugs to suppress their immune systems a bit, to allow the new organ or bone marrow to work in the body. The problem is, these drugs also prevent the immune system from doing its usual job of fighting germs. This means that transplant patients are very vulnerable to germs that healthy people have no trouble fighting off.

It appears that this is what happened in Garrett's case. In mid-April 1997, he contracted an infection and, as a result of his weakened condition, he died shortly after.

Mia was heart-broken. Garrett had meant so much to her and had been partially responsible for her present fame and fortune.

"I would give it all up in a heart beat to have him back," she said. "Just to give him one more day or one more week. But I know Garrett wouldn't want that . . . Now, no matter where I play, I know Garrett will be there."

Although she was devastated by the loss of her brother, Mia also knew that Garrett would want her to keep on playing. A few weeks after his death, she returned to the team to continue the soccer season. Her commitment to the game and the support of her teammates made it easier to deal with her grief.

In May, the team played in two international contests that were televised nationally. Mia scored three goals in each game. Team USA hosted the 1997 US Women's Cup that summer and every player wore a black armband in Garrett's honor. Throughout the season Mia scored 18 goals in 16 games. For the fourth consecutive year, she was named the US Soccer Federation's Female Athlete of the Year for her efforts.

The year 1998 was full of new challenges and new goals. Aside from her demanding training and game schedule, Mia was doing more and more work promoting her sport throughout the country. She was convinced that in order to really improve the overall soccer situation in America, a professional women's soccer league, similar to the men's Major League Soccer, was needed. To develop continuing interest and provide development opportunities for the national team, a wider base of talented players was needed than what the college system alone could provide. A professional soccer league would offer more women players the opportunity to develop and maintain their skills while earning a living. This would provide a large pool of talented players from which to draw on for international competitions.

Many countries already had such programs in place. Since the Olympics, European countries in particular were providing more resources to their women's teams, and professional teams were already established in a number of countries. Throughout the 1990s a number of American players, like Michelle Akers, had actually played for a period of time in European professional leagues in order to stay competitive.

The national team was focusing on the upcoming 1999 Women's World Cup the following summer. In the meantime it had the satisfaction of beating Norway again 3-0 in the final of the International Women's Tournament.

During the following Goodwill Games, Mia scored three goals against the Danes in the semi-final. Then she went on to score two goals in the final against China, to give the US the gold medal with a decisive 2-0 victory. At the end of the season, Mia had 20 goals and 20 assists in 20 games.

One of the most satisfying moments of the year for Mia occurred that fall with the launch of the Mia Hamm Foundation. The twin missions of the organization were to fund research into a cure for aplastic anemia, the debilitating disease that had affected Garrett and so many other people; and to promote and to provide opportunities for young women to excel in sports.

With the help of her teammates, Mia began an annual soccer game fund-raiser called the Garrett Game that teamed national club players against an All-Star college team to raise money for bone marrow transplant research. The first game of this event raised $150,000.

The 1999 season was demanding for the national team as they prepared for the summer World Cup. They were under considerable pressure to demonstrate they were capable of winning the upcoming tournament. The team did well, although Mia experienced a worrying eight-game scoring drought in the spring. As the team's star striker, Mia knew she was expected to score goals. However, many star performers face similar challenges as they deal with determined efforts by their opponents to shut them down.

In May, in a game against the Netherlands, Mia overcame her dry spell to tie the record of 107 goals scored in international competition set by famous Italian player Elizabetta Vignotto. In a rough and tumble game against Brazil a few weeks later, she became the all-time leading scorer in the history of international soccer when she scored the 108th goal of her career.

The beautifully executed goal was set in motion when Michelle Akers lofted a ball to Mia about 40 yards (36 m) from the net. Hamm headed the ball to Kristine Lilly, who slipped a pass to Cindy Parlow in front of the penalty box. Parlow passed the ball back to Mia as she cut towards the goal. Mia burst into the right side of the penalty box. She fought off a defender, then kicked the ball through the legs of the Brazilian goalkeeper from 10 yards (9 m) out to make history.

The goal cleared the Team USA bench as they swarmed onto the field to congratulate Mia. Team captain Carla Overbeck retrieved the ball and presented it to Mia with the good wishes of all her teammates.

After the game Mia said, "It was special to get the record on such a great team goal."

As the summer approached, World Cup fever began to build. Credit for much of the excitement went to Marla Messing and Donna de Varona, the two leaders of the organizing committee that was overseeing the games. They had contributed to the success of the Men's World Cup in 1994 and were confident the 1999 Women's World Cup would be an even bigger event. They convinced FIFA to book the best stadiums across America for the tournament.

The attendance records for the games even surpassed the expectations of the committee organizers. They had hoped to sell 325,000 tickets, but the final numbers were over 650,000 paying customers throughout the 16-game tournament. Over two and a half million people watched the games on television in America, and many millions more tuned in around the world.

More corporations became interested in working with Mia and other national players to promote their products. Mia was soon making over a million dollars a year from endorsements. The Gatorade company even produced an TV commercial featuring Mia and Michael Jordan. It showed the superstars squaring off in a series of sport contests that end when Mia sends Michael flying with a judo flip.

Now other team members with less of a profile than

Mia were being paid to make public appearances as well. The players began referring affectionately to this income as "Mia's money." While grateful for the over-due financial rewards, Mia remained a reserved, self-deprecating athlete.

At the World Cup tournament, Team USA got off to a shaky start against Denmark in the first game of the series. Perhaps too anxious, the team made sloppy passes and had trouble co-ordinating their plays. Mia settled the team down with a blazing goal in the first 17 minutes of play. Ten minutes later, Mia sent a hard cross from the right side to Julie Foudy, who drove the ball into the goal.

After that, the team relaxed and scored twice more to win their opener 3-0. Team USA went on to win in their group and ended up facing China for the Cup.

The final game of the 1999 Women's World Cup was held in the famous Rose Bowl in Pasadena, California. When the teams arrived on the field, the stadium was packed with just over 90,000 cheering fans, the largest crowd to attend a women's sports event — ever.

Although the Americans were favored to win, the Chinese were believed to have the stronger offence. Both teams played strong defensive games, knowing that the slightest error could be fatal. Michelle Akers, probably playing in her last World Cup, did a superb job co-ordinating the American defence. The two teams had played together so many times over the years that the players could almost predict each other's moves. There were exciting moments in front of the goals, but neither team was able to complete their chances.

Late in the game, battling for a corner kick in front of her own goal, Michelle Akers ran into goalie Biana Scurry and had to be helped off the field. Sensing an advantage, the Chinese pressed in more intensely. But they were held in check by a determined American defence.

The game went into two 15-minute periods of regulation overtime. Both teams kept up their offensive efforts, but neither was able to come up with the golden goal. China almost scored from a corner kick when forward Fan Yunjie headed the ball through Scurry's hands. Fortunately, Kristine Lilly was against the near post and cleared the ball out of the goal area to save the day.

"Just doing my job," she commented later.

At the end of overtime both sides were still scoreless. As there can be no ties in international championship games, the winner had to be decided in penalty kicks. Each team would get five direct shots on the goal from 12 yards (11 m) out. The team with the most goals would take the World Cup.

No team likes games being decided in penalty kicks. Such a contest does not decide who is the better team — only who is going to be declared the winner. After such an intense game it was frustrating and disappointing to have the winner decided in this fashion. However, those are the rules. Team USA stayed focused and prepared for the shoot-out.

The first two kickers on each team scored easily. Then Scurry made a spectacular save by deflecting a shot from Liu Ying. Now the Americans had the edge. All the other kickers, including Mia, made their shots good. The score was 4-4. Now it came down the last shot by Brandi Chastain.

Everything rested on this one kick. Despite the intense pressure, Chastain rose to the moment. She drove the ball into the left side of the net to win the World Cup. She was so excited she dropped to her knees, tore her jersey off, and waved it over her head as the crowed roared its approval. For the second time in the decade, America had won the Women's World Cup.

The crowd kept up its roar as huge clouds of confetti drifted across the field. The Team USA players hugged, wept, and congratulated each other, and then turned to the crowd to show their appreciation.

Perhaps Coach DiCicco summed it up best after the game when he said, "This is a team of courage. There were so many things they had to overcome. They fought and fought and fought to win this tournament. Most of all they were up against an outstanding China team. To my mind, there are two champions here . . .

there is only one that is taking the World Cup. America should be proud."

In the months following the World Cup win Mia and her teammates were more in demand than ever. Requests for interviews and appearances flooded in from across the United States and around the world. Mia and other team members showed up on television on David Letterman's *Late Night* show. *Sports Illustrated* featured the team on the cover of the magazine in the fall. Mia was becoming so popular she represented the possibilities for women in all sports, not just soccer.

As Team USA began to prepare to defend their gold medal at the 2000 Summer Olympics in Sydney, Australia, Mia and her teammates continued their campaign to increase the popularity of soccer in America, in particular with young girls.

"We want to get girls out to the games," Mia says. "We want them to see the chemistry and the intensity. Our success is as a team, not as an individual."

Although Mia is an exemplary team player, the strength of the team has much to do with her extraordinary individual talent and determination. Whatever the future holds for Mia Hamm, she will be the ideal example of sportsmanship for a long time to come.

Glossary of Soccer Terms

advantage: a situation in which an offence has been committed, usually by a defensive player, but the referee allows the game to continue (as long as the offensive team has possession of the ball) so that the offending team does not gain an advantage.

assist: a pass from one player to another that leads to a goal. Some people think this pass is as important as the goal itself.

attacker: any player who is in the opponent's half of the field.

banana kick: kicking the ball hard with the inside or outside of your foot so the ball curves around a defender or goalkeeper.

breakaway: when a player has the ball and breaks through defenders to confront the goalkeeper one on one.

center circle: the marked circle, with a radius of 10 feet (9.15 m) at the center of the field. The center of this circle is called the **center mark**.

changing the field: a pass that takes the ball from the side of the field where there are a lot of players to the other side of the field that is less crowded.

charging: shoulder-to-shoulder contact between players as they fight for possession of the ball. The object is to put the other player slightly off balance. If charging is done too roughly you can get a foul.

chip: a short pass that pops the ball over the heads of defenders.

corner area: the marked area (a quarter circle with a radius of 1 yard [1 m]) in each of the four corners of the field. This is the area from which the corner kicks must be taken.

corner kick: a direct free kick awarded to the offensive team when the last player to touch the ball before it crosses the base or goal line is a defending player. During a corner kick offensive players cannot be offside. The corner kick is taken from the **corner area.**

cross: a long kick, usually in the air, from one side of the field to the other.

dead ball: occurs when the referee stops a game due to a foul or other infraction of the rules. If play is stopped because of a foul, the ball is put back into play from the spot where the infraction took place.

defender: any player in his or her own half of the field.

direct free kick: a free kick from a dead ball position from which a goal can be scored.

dribbling: moving the ball around the field with your feet while keeping it under control.

drop ball: method used by the referee to restart play after a game has been stopped for a reason other than an offence by a player. The referee drops the ball between players from each team. The ball must hit the ground before it can be played.

extra time: an additional period of time after regulation play to decide a game that is a tie or draw.

far post: the goal post farthest way from the offensive player in possession of the ball.

flick pass: a short quick pass from the side of the foot, usually done while dribbling.

foul: any action that breaks the rules of the game. For a minor foul, the opposite team gets an indirect kick. For a major foul in the penalty area, the opposite team gets a penalty kick.

goal area: the marked area, 6 yards by 20 yards (5.5 by 18.3 m), in front of each goal.

goalkeeper (goalie, keeper, net minder): the principal player on each team who guards the goal. The goalkeeper is the only player who can handle the ball within his or her penalty area.

goal kick: a kick by a defending team that restarts play when the ball is put over the base or goal line, outside of the goal, by an attacking team.

goal line, base line: the line on which the goal posts stand; it runs the length of each end of the soccer field.

goal mouth: the area immediately in front of the goal.

golden goal: the goal that determines the winner in a tie game that goes into overtime. The first goal scored in overtime play that decides the winner and ends the game.

halfway line: line that runs across the center of the field.

hand ball; handling: the intentional use of the hands or arms to direct the ball. Handling is a major foul.

hat trick: a player scores three goals in the same game.

heading: to hit the ball with some part of the head, usually the front or side, in order to pass or score.

holding: the intentional use the hands or arms to obstruct an opposing player from playing the game.

indirect free kick: a kick from a dead ball position taken after a minor foul. The ball must be touched by another player from either side before a goal can be scored.

instep kick: to kick the ball with the top of your foot where the shoe laces are. This results in a powerful, accurate, straight shot.

kick off: the kick from the center mark that starts a game or restarts play after a goal is scored. The ball must go forward its full circumference before it can be touched by another player.

marking: to guard an opponent closely.

misconduct: any behavior during a game that is considered by the referee to be contrary to the intention or spirit of the Laws of the Game.

near post: the post closest to an attacker with the ball.

nutmeg: when you dribble a ball though an opposing player's legs and pick it up again on the other side. An embarrassing moment for the defending player.

obstruction/impeding: infraction that occurs when any player, either in possession of the ball or not, acts in a way that hinders the progress of the game.

offside: probably the most frequent foul in soccer. Offsides occur when an attacking player without the ball is between the last defender and the goal keeper. To avoid being offside there has to be two defending players between an attacking player and the goal. If the ball is ahead of the attacking player at the moment it is played, the player is not offside.

outswinger: a corner kick that curves away from the goal mouth. This kind of kick can pull the goalkeeper out of position.

overhead kick, bicycle kick: kicking the ball backwards over one's head. A difficult and dangerous maneuver, it should only be tried by experienced players.

own goal: goal accidentally scored against one's own team. Probably the most embarrassing soccer moment for any player.

penalty arc: the marked semi-circular area on top of the penalty area. It indicates the 10-yard (9-m) distance from the penalty mark that all players except the kicker and goalkeeper must keep during a penalty kick

penalty area: the larger marked area, 16 yards by 36 yards (16.5 m by 43.3 m) in front of each goal, where the goalkeeper is allowed to handle the ball.

penalty kick: a direct free kick awarded to the attacking team when an attacking player is fouled while in a good position to score.

penalty mark: penalty shots are taken from this spot right in front of the goal, 12 yards (11 m) out from the goal line.

pitch: the British term for a soccer field.

red card: card held up by the referee to indicate that a player or coach has been ejected from a game. Also called being ejected or sent off. It usually occurs after a yellow card has been issued for serious misconduct. The player's number is recorded and later league officials may impose fines or suspensions depending on the seriousness of the offence.

referee: the principal game official responsible for the conduct of the game. The referee makes decisions on infractions and the rules of the game.

result: the final score at the end of a soccer game. The team with the most goals is the winner. If there is no score or each side has the same number of goals the game is a "draw" or "tie."

save: a player, usually the goalkeeper but not always, who is credited with blocking a goal.

sliding tackle: an often desperate and difficult tactic to get the ball away from an attacker. The defender slides at the ball with one or both feet in an attempt to kick the ball. If the attacker is tripped after the ball has been touched it is not a foul.

square pass: usually a short or medium pass directly across the field to an open teammate.

striker: the forwards who are in the best position to strike at the goal.

substitute: an extra player who can replace a player on the field.

sudden death overtime: method of determining winners for tied games. Almost all international games that are tied are decided in this manner. The first team to score in this type of overtime is the winner of the game.

through pass: a kick that sends the ball between defenders or over their heads. The ball should land in such a way that it is retrievable by an offensive player but not by the defending goalkeeper.

throw-in: method of returning the ball to play after it goes out of bounds over the touch/side lines. The opposite team from the player who last touched the ball before it went over the line gets to restart play with a throw-in. The player puts the ball back into play with a two-handed, over-the-head throw. A goal cannot be scored from a throw-in unless the ball touches another player first.

tie-breaker: a system used in some tournaments or international games where, after regulation overtime there is still no winner, a set number of direct kicks on goal take place from the penalty mark to determine the winner.

touch or side line: the boundary line on each side of the soccer field.

trapping: stopping the ball with your body in such a way that the ball falls gently to the ground at your feet. This is done by letting your body "give" just the right amount when the ball hits you.

volleying: kicking the ball while it is still in the air.

volley kick: a kick that goes a long distance, usually done by the defensive players to get the ball into the opponent's side of the field.

wall: a line of defensive players in front of the goal in an effort to block a free kick close to their goal.

World Cup: organized by FIFA every four years, this international soccer tournament includes the best national teams in the world.

yellow card, caution: the referee holds up a yellow card if a player commits a serious foul or other misconduct.

Research Sources

Books

Christopher, Matt. *On the Field with...Mia Hamm*. New York: Little, Brown and Company, 1998.

Hamm, Mia (with Aaron Heifetz). *Go for the Goal: A Champion's Guide to Winning at Soccer and Life*. New York: Harper Collins Publishers, 1999.

Jarman, John. *Junior Soccer: A Guide for Teachers and Young Soccer Players*. London: Faber and Faber, 1976.

Marshall, David. *Soccer*. Crystal Lake, IL: Rigby Interactive Library (Reed Elsevier Inc.), 1997.

Rutledge, Rachel. *Women of Sports. The Best of the Best in Soccer*. Brookfield, Conn.: Millbrook Press, 1998.

Sakurai, Jennifer. *Soccer: The Rules of the Game*. Los Angeles: Price Stern Sloan, 1990.

Stewart, Mark. *Mia Hamm: Good as Gold*. New York: Children's Press, (Grolier Publishing Co.), 1999.

Internet Resources

www.miafoundation.org
-The website for Mia's foundation which funds bone marrow transplant research and the promotion of sports for young women.

home.beseen.com
-Excellent site for current information on Mia Hamm and Team USA

www.us-soccer.com
-The official site of the US Soccer Federation

www.womensoccer.com
-A magazine devoted to coverage of international women's soccer.

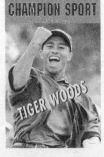

We hope you have enjoyed this
CHAMPION SPORT Biography.

We welcome your comments and sugges-
tions.

Please contact us at

Warwick Publishing

162 John Street
Toronto, Ontario, Canada
M5V 2E5

Telephone: (416) 596-1555

FAX: (416) 596-1520

E-Mail:
mbrooke@warwickgp.com

— • —

Please visit our Web site at

www.warwickgp.com